T0007913

The True Story of Annette Kellerman, World-Class
Swimmer, Fashion Pioneer, and Real-Life Mermaid

Annette
Feels Free

Katie Mazeika

Beach Lane Books

New York   London   Toronto   Sydney   New Delhi

The entire city was abuzz. There was a real-life mermaid swimming and dancing with the fish in Australia's Melbourne Aquarium! Her name was Annette Kellerman, but the newspapers called her "The Original Mermaid." Everyone wanted to see the girl who danced underwater.

Annette was born in a land filled with sunshine, into a home filled with music. She twirled and pirouetted while her parents played beautiful melodies. When she danced, she felt free.

But when Annette was six, her legs became weak and her steps became wobbly. She may have had polio, or it could have been rickets. No one really knows. A doctor gave her braces to wear. Annette hated the braces; they felt like hot cages on her legs.

There were no more leaps or graceful
pirouettes, just clumsy turns and awkward
steps. Annette stopped dancing.

Annette's parents worried. Their daughter never sang or laughed like she used to.

They played her favorite songs.

They read her favorite stories.

But Annette remained still and silent.

Then one day her father had an idea. . . .

He took off Annette's braces and carried her into Lavender Bay.

Annette loved the cool freedom of the ocean. She laughed and danced in the waves, kicking her legs. *Splash, splash!* In the water, Annette felt free again.

Annette kicked

and danced

and swam . . .

until she became the strongest swimmer in New South
Wales! The more she swam, the stronger her legs
became, and the less she needed her braces.

Annette kept swimming, competing, and dancing underwater. She performed water ballets with flips, kicks, and jumps for delighted spectators and overflowing audiences as news of her water dancing spread. When she raced, she broke every long-distance swimming record in Australia.

In England there would be more people, bigger theaters, and longer races.
So Annette went off to break new barriers and set new records there.

Annette dove into a glass tank at the London Hippodrome in front of hundreds of people. Then she danced in the water. The crowds were astounded. The press dubbed her "The Diving Venus," after the Roman goddess who was believed to have risen from the sea.

Annette wanted to be the first woman to swim across the English Channel. She earned the support of a London newspaper and a chocolatier. They gave her an endless supply of hot cocoa to drink while she swam—a good thing, because she needed energy to get through the all-day swim.

But Annette was expected to wear a cumbersome swimsuit while the men who tried to swim the channel were allowed to swim naked! The suit chafed and weighed Annette down in the choppy ocean waters. Despite this, Annette made it three-quarters of the way across.

Annette and her father traveled throughout Europe. There, Annette competed in swim races, not just against other women, but against men, too. And she won! The crowds were agog. They called her "Australia's Champion Lady Swimmer." No woman had ever raced against men—let alone won.

Annette was invited to America. Crowds traveled across the
states to see Annette dance in the water and compete in races.

But the more Annette swam, the more she struggled with her swim costume. Because she was a woman, she still had to perform and compete in a full skirt and pantaloons. They felt like cages around her legs and reminded her of her braces. Why should she compete against men with her legs in cages while their legs were kicking free?

Annette decided to sew her own swim costume.

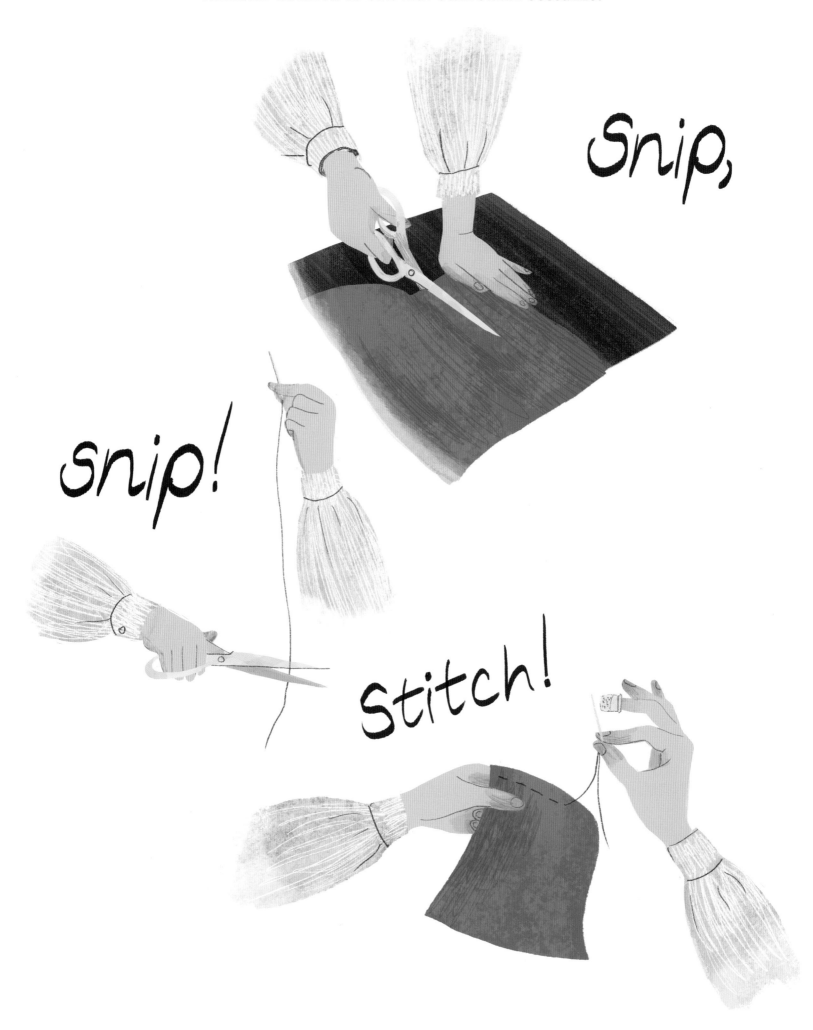

Wearing it reminded her of the cool freedom she felt that first time she swam at home in Lavender Bay.

Ahhhh! *This* was how she wanted to dance and swim in the water from now on. No big skirt, no pantaloons, just freedom.

Annette put on her new swimming costume and set off for Revere Beach in Boston. She had a race coming up and needed to train. But when she stepped onto the beach in her new swimsuit, a cry of shock echoed through the crowd. Then a policeman arrested Annette for not wearing enough clothing!

Annette went to court. She didn't want to swim in skirts and pantaloons ever again! She argued that she should be allowed the same freedom when she swam as her male opponents.

The judge saw the logic in Annette's argument, so the charges were dismissed. Annette was allowed to wear her swimsuit. But there was one condition. She had to cover up with a cape all the way to the edge of the water.

Annette's new swimsuit became known as the "Annette Kellerman,"
and fashionable women everywhere ditched their skirts and pantaloons
for the cool freedom of bare knees. As time went by, and as the suits—
and swimming—became more popular, even capes were no longer required.

Annette continued racing, diving, and water dancing in shows all over the world. She even starred in fourteen movies! Eventually, she returned to Australia to train young women in diving and "ornamental swimming." She called them her "Kellermanettes," and they appeared with her in charity performances across Australia and the United States.

Today, female athletes from around the world still dance in the water.
It's called "artistic swimming" and is part of the Summer Olympics.

Women competing in swim races now have streamlined suits that don't hold them back in the water. And women just taking a swim are allowed to wear whatever they feel good in.

All thanks to a girl named Annette,
who wanted to feel free.

MORE ON ANNETTE KELLERMAN

There are many stories to be told of Annette Kellerman's life. There is the story of a fearless champion swimmer who shattered swimming and diving records. Although still a teenager, Annette held almost every swim record in Australia by the time she left for England. She caught the world's attention and became one of the first celebrity athletes. Annette used that fame to help make swimming not just an acceptable and popular sport for women, but a vital skill.

Then there is the story of Annette the performer. As a teen, she began appearing in underwater ballets at a local aquarium and went on to wow crowds all over the world. She performed on Broadway in New York City and on vaudeville stages across France and starred in more than a dozen

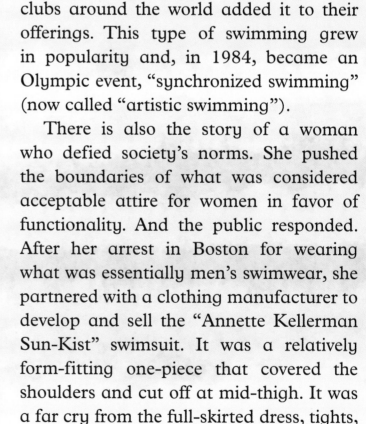

Press photograph of Annette wearing her famous suit

movies. She was one of Hollywood's first starlets and has a star on the Hollywood Walk of Fame. A movie was even made about her life: *Million Dollar Mermaid* (1952), with fellow swimmer-actress Esther Williams starring as Annette.

Center stage in all her performances was Annette's "ornamental swimming," a new art form that she continued to develop throughout her career. She went on to teach it to others, and by the 1920s, swim clubs around the world added it to their offerings. This type of swimming grew in popularity and, in 1984, became an Olympic event, "synchronized swimming" (now called "artistic swimming").

There is also the story of a woman who defied society's norms. She pushed the boundaries of what was considered acceptable attire for women in favor of functionality. And the public responded. After her arrest in Boston for wearing what was essentially men's swimwear, she partnered with a clothing manufacturer to develop and sell the "Annette Kellerman Sun-Kist" swimsuit. It was a relatively form-fitting one-piece that covered the shoulders and cut off at mid-thigh. It was a far cry from the full-skirted dress, tights, shoes, and cap that women had previously been required to wear to swim.

Lastly, there is Annette the character,

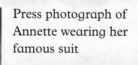

her favorite role. She loved to tell and retell stories of her life, and each time, the details were grander, the distances longer, and the heights higher. Often her embellishments were unnecessary; for instance, she really did dive off a seventy-foot cliff for one film and into a pool of alligators for another. She was always performing and playing to her audience. She gave fans what they wanted: a figure larger than life.

Of all the stories of Annette, the one that stands out most is the story of a woman who pushed boundaries and advanced women's rights. And we can all thank Annette for the freedom of wearing what we feel best in at the beach.

Newspaper photograph of Annette stopping to drink cocoa while swimming the English Channel

AUTHOR'S NOTE

I lost my right eye to cancer just before my third birthday. That surgery led to many more surgeries and a lifelong seizure disorder. As much as I hated being the kid with the eye patch all through school, and as much as I struggled through early adulthood to accept myself rather than being embarrassed by my disability, I believe that being different from my peers growing up shaped my life. I wouldn't be who I am, nor would I likely be doing this job today, if I hadn't gotten sick decades ago. Had Annette never gotten sick, it's likely that she never would have learned to swim. Through swimming, Annette not only found something she excelled at, but she found her voice and her passion, both of which she used to make positive changes in her life and in the lives of countless others. Looking back on her childhood, Annette considered her disability to be a transformative experience, going so far as to call it her "greatest blessing." Not everyone can leave their disability behind like Annette did. But Annette's experience with disability shaped who she was and how she dealt with limitations. And it was because of those experiences that she became a force in the history of swimming and women's rights.

To my mom, who showed me that women
can do anything, and to my dad, who always
knew I was a writer (even when I didn't)

Sources

Donnelly, Marea. "From Cripple to Star: How Annette Kellerman Became a 'Pinnacle of Physical Feminine Perfection.'" *Daily Telegraph* (Sydney), August 8, 2016.

Johns, Isabel. "Boston Arrest a Mistake, Says Annette." *Boston Sunday Globe*, October 11, 1953.

Kellerman, Annette. *How to Swim.* New York: George H. Doran, 1918.

Walsh, G. P. "Kellerman, Annette Marie Sarah (1886–1975)." In *Australian Dictionary of Biography, Volume 9: 1891–1939.* Melbourne University Press, 1983.

Wilkes-Barre Times Leader, The Evening News. "Annette Is a Mermaid, Beautiful and Strong." August 11, 1908.

Winnipeg Tribune. "Swimming the Channel." August 23, 1906.

BEACH LANE BOOKS • An imprint of Simon & Schuster Children's Publishing Division • 1230 Avenue of the Americas, New York, New York 10020 • © 2022 by Katie Mazeika • Book design by Rebecca Syracuse © 2022 by Simon & Schuster, Inc. • All rights reserved, including the right of reproduction in whole or in part in any form. • BEACH LANE BOOKS and colophon are trademarks of Simon & Schuster, Inc. • For information about special discounts for bulk purchases, please contact Simon & Schuster Special Sales at 1-866-506-1949 or business@simonandschuster.com. • The Simon & Schuster Speakers Bureau can bring authors to your live event. For more information or to book an event, contact the Simon & Schuster Speakers Bureau at 1-866-248-3049 or visit our website at www.simonspeakers.com. • The text for this book was set in Plantin Infant MT Std. • The illustrations for this book were rendered digitally. • Manufactured in China • 0522 SCP • First Edition • 10 9 8 7 6 5 4 3 2 1 • Library of Congress Cataloging-in-Publication Data • Names: Mazeika, Katie, author. • Title: Annette feels free : the true story of Annette Kellerman, world-class swimmer, fashion pioneer, and real-life mermaid / Katie Mazeika. • Description: First edition. | New York : Beach Lane Books, [2022] | Includes bibliographical references. | Audience: Ages 0-8 | Audience: Grades 2-3 | Summary: "Meet 'The Original Mermaid,' Annette Kellerman! All her life, Annette wanted one thing: to feel free. As a girl she found freedom in the water, where she could swim without the leg braces she needed on land. As she grew up, Annette swam in Australia and England and America and beyond, performing synchronized swimming—which she invented!—and competing in swim races and diving exhibitions. But always she was bogged down by her heavy swim clothes. Clothes that only women had to wear, not men. So Annette designed her own swim costume. And then, she fought for the right to wear it—and for the right for all women to feel free"— Provided by publisher. • Identifiers: LCCN 2021062174 (print) | LCCN 2021062175 (ebook) | ISBN 9781665903431 (hardcover) | ISBN 9781665903448 (ebook) • Subjects: LCSH: Kellerman, Annette, 1886–1975—Juvenile literature. | Women swimmers—Australia—Biography—Juvenile literature. | Swimmers—Australia—Biography—Juvenile literature. | Athletes with disabilities—Australia—Biography—Juvenile literature. • Classification: LCC GV838.K45 M39 2022 (print) | LCC GV838.K45 (ebook) | DDC 797.2/1092 [B]—dc23/eng/20220126 • LC record available at https://lccn.loc.gov/2021062174 • LC ebook record available at https://lccn.loc.gov/2021062175